The CEO's

31-Day Power Plan:
Unlocking Success through Essential Traits

Gerard Assey

The CEO's 31-Day Power Plan:
Unlocking Success through Essential Traits

By

Gerard Assey

Published by:
Gerard Assey
19/18, Palli Arasan Street
Anna Nagar East
Chennai - 600 102

ISBN: 978-93-92492-74-7

(Image courtesy: mhouge from Pixabay at: 'https://www.pixabay.com' Thank You)

Table of Contents

Preface

Welcome to **'The CEO's 31-Day Power Plan: Unlocking Success through Essential Traits'**- a book designed to empower CEOs and aspiring leaders with a comprehensive guide to developing the essential attributes that drive success. In today's dynamic and ever-evolving business landscape, the role of a CEO demands a diverse skill set and a keen understanding of what it takes to lead with excellence.

This book is born out of a deep belief in the transformative power of personal development. Each day, over the course of a month, we will explore one key trait essential for CEOs to cultivate and integrate into their leadership journey. From visionary thinking and strategic mindset to effective communication and resilience, each trait plays a vital role in shaping exceptional leadership.

Through detailed explanations, real-life examples, and actionable insights, this book will provide you with the tools and knowledge to enhance your leadership capabilities. We firmly believe that by embracing these traits, CEOs can unlock their full potential, inspire their teams, drive organizational growth, and make a lasting impact.

The structure of this book allows for a daily exploration of each trait, enabling you to focus on one attribute at a time. By dedicating yourself to this journey, you will embark on a transformative experience that will expand your horizons, challenge your perspectives, and elevate your leadership prowess.

We encourage you to approach this book with an open mind, ready to embrace change, growth, and self-reflection. Take each day as an opportunity to learn, reflect, and apply the knowledge gained. The journey may present challenges, but it is through perseverance and dedication that true growth and transformation occur.

As you embark on this 31-day exploration of essential CEO traits, we wish you great success and fulfillment. May this book serve as a valuable companion on your path to becoming an exceptional leader, one trait at a time.
Remember, the power to unlock your true leadership potential lies within you.

Let the journey begin NOW!

How to Effectively Use this Book to Make the Most of the 31-Day Essential Journey

1. Familiarize Yourself: Read through the book to understand the structure, content, and purpose of each essential trait.
2. Set Clear Intentions: Define your objectives for this 31-day journey. What do you hope to gain? How do you envision incorporating these traits into your leadership style?
3. Daily Focus: Allocate dedicated time each day to delve into the specific trait highlighted for that day. Create a routine that suits your schedule and allows for deep reflection and exploration.
4. Absorb the Information: Take your time to absorb the information presented. Read the explanations, examples, and practical insights provided for each trait. Consider how they apply to your current leadership role and challenges.
5. Reflect: Engage in self-reflection after reading about each trait. Consider your strengths and areas for improvement related to that particular attribute. Reflect on how you can enhance your leadership by embodying that trait.
6. Action Planning: Develop an action plan to integrate the trait into your leadership approach. Identify specific behaviors, strategies, or practices you can adopt to reinforce the trait in your daily activities.

7. Seek Accountability: Share your journey with a trusted mentor, coach, or colleague. Regularly discuss your progress, challenges, and insights with them. Their guidance and support can further enrich your experience.
8. Apply and Practice: Actively apply the trait throughout the day, both in professional and personal interactions. Look for opportunities to demonstrate the trait's qualities and observe the impact it has on yourself and others.
9. Reflect on Progress: At the end of each day, reflect on how you applied the trait and the outcomes achieved. Consider the lessons learned and how you can further refine your approach moving forward.
10. Engage in Self-Celebration: Acknowledge your progress and successes. Celebrate the milestones and growth you experience along the way. This positivity and self-recognition will reinforce your commitment to developing these essential traits.
11. Continuous Learning: Embrace the idea that this journey is not confined to 31 days. Commit to lifelong learning and growth. Look for additional resources, workshops, or learning opportunities to deepen your understanding of the traits.
12. Apply the Traits Synergistically: As you progress through the 31 traits, strive to integrate them synergistically. Recognize the interconnectedness of these attributes and how they collectively shape your leadership approach.
13. Share Insights and Inspire Others: Throughout the journey, share your insights, experiences,

and lessons learned with your team, colleagues, or wider professional network. Inspire others to embark on their own leadership development journeys.

14. Review and Reflect: Once you complete the 31-day journey, review your action plans, reflections, and the overall impact of the experience. Consider how these essential traits have shaped your leadership style and identify areas for further growth.
15. Continuous Development: Commit to ongoing development by revisiting the traits periodically, integrating them into your leadership practices, and continuing to refine your skills and capabilities as a CEO.

By following these step-by-step tips, you as the CEO can make the most of this 31-day essential traits journey, developing your leadership skills, and creating lasting positive change within yourself and your organization.

Why do CEO's Fail? Factors that Derail the Success and How to Prevent them

CEO failure can occur due to a variety of factors, ranging from internal issues to external market forces. Some key factors that can derail a CEO's climb or success include:

- ✓ Poor Leadership: Ineffective leadership skills, such as a lack of strategic vision, an inability to inspire and motivate teams, or a failure to adapt to changing circumstances, can lead to CEO failure.

  Example: Consider Alex Beacon, the CEO of a once-thriving virtual reality gaming company, Quantum Odyssey. Despite a promising start, Beacon's leadership faltered. He struggled to envision the next phase in gaming technology, failed to inspire innovation among the team, and overlooked the rising popularity of augmented reality. The company faced a downturn as competitors embraced these trends, ultimately leading to Beacon's departure.
- ✓ Lack of Emotional Intelligence: Emotional intelligence, including self-awareness, empathy, and the ability to manage relationships, is crucial for effective leadership. CEOs who lack emotional intelligence may struggle to connect with their teams, make poor decisions based on emotions rather than facts, or fail to build strong relationships with stakeholders.

Example: Meet Morgan Hale, the CEO of FutureTech Solutions. Despite being a tech prodigy, Hale's lack of emotional intelligence became evident. During crucial board meetings, Hale's decisions were driven more by personal emotions than strategic analysis. This strained relationships with key stakeholders, including the board and employees, resulting in a loss of trust. The board eventually decided that the company needed a leader who could connect emotionally with the team.

- ✓ Inadequate Succession Planning: Failing to plan for the long-term leadership of the company can disrupt continuity and hinder success. CEOs who neglect succession planning may leave the organization without a suitable successor or fail to adequately prepare the next generation of leaders. *Example:* Imagine the case of Olivia Vanguard, CEO of Stellar Innovations. Caught up in the daily operations and immediate goals, Vanguard neglected succession planning. When she unexpectedly decided to retire, the company found itself without a clear successor. The lack of a smooth transition disrupted operations, causing a decline in shareholder confidence and contributing to the company's struggles.
- ✓ Lack of Accountability: CEOs must take responsibility for their actions and decisions. When CEOs fail to hold themselves accountable or fail to create a culture of accountability within the organization, it can lead to poor decision-making, unethical

behavior, and a lack of transparency. *Example:* Consider Blake Summit, CEO of Pinnacle Pharma. Summit's tenure was marred by a lack of accountability. When a major product recall occurred due to manufacturing issues, Summit failed to take responsibility. The absence of a transparent communication strategy and a refusal to acknowledge the problem resulted in a loss of credibility. Shareholders and the board, dissatisfied with the lack of accountability, initiated a leadership change.

✓ Failure to Adapt to Market Changes: The business landscape is constantly evolving, and CEOs who fail to adapt to market changes risk becoming irrelevant.
Example: Think of Casey Swift, CEO of Apex Motors. In an era of increasing emphasis on electric vehicles, Swift, focused on traditional gasoline cars, failed to adapt. Ignoring the market shift, Apex Motors lost ground to competitors embracing sustainable technology. Swift's reluctance to recognize the changing automotive landscape contributed significantly to the company's financial decline and eventual acquisition by a forward-thinking competitor.

To prevent these factors from derailing CEO success, several strategies can be implemented:

✓ Continuous Learning and Development: CEOs should invest in their own growth and development, seeking out opportunities to enhance their leadership skills, emotional intelligence, and industry knowledge.

Engaging in executive education programs, mentorship, and networking can help CEOs stay relevant and adaptable.

- ✓ Building a Strong Leadership Team: CEOs should surround themselves with capable and diverse leaders who can complement their skills and compensate for their weaknesses. This team should be aligned with the CEO's vision, possess complementary expertise, and share a commitment to the organization's success.
- ✓ Creating a Culture of Accountability: CEOs should foster a culture of transparency, open communication, and accountability within the organization. They should lead by example, setting high ethical standards and holding themselves and others accountable for their actions and decisions.
- ✓ Embracing Change and Innovation: CEOs must stay attuned to market trends and proactively adapt their strategies and operations to remain competitive. Embracing innovation, encouraging experimentation, and fostering a culture of continuous improvement can help CEOs navigate market changes effectively.
- ✓ Succession Planning and Talent Development: CEOs should prioritize succession planning, identifying and grooming potential successors within the organization. Developing a talent pipeline ensures a smooth leadership transition and maintains continuity in the face of change.

By addressing these key factors and implementing preventive measures, CEOs can mitigate the risks that may lead to failure and increase their chances of long-term success.

Importance of a CEO Investing in Self-Development and Personal Growth

Investing in self-development and continuously building on key attributes is of paramount importance for a CEO. Here are several reasons why a CEO should prioritize their personal growth:

1. Enhancing Leadership Effectiveness: A CEO's leadership skills directly impact the success of the organization. By investing in personal development, CEOs can enhance their leadership capabilities, inspire their teams, and drive organizational growth. They can develop the skills and mindset necessary to effectively navigate challenges, make informed decisions, and lead with confidence.
2. Adapting to a Changing Business Landscape: The business landscape is constantly evolving, driven by technological advancements, market shifts, and changing customer expectations. CEOs need to stay ahead of these changes and adapt their strategies accordingly. Investing in self-development allows CEOs to stay updated with industry trends, acquire new knowledge and skills, and embrace innovation and change.
3. Fostering Personal Growth and Fulfillment: Personal growth goes hand in hand with professional growth. CEOs who invest in their personal development experience a sense of fulfillment, self-awareness, and continuous

improvement. This personal growth not only benefits their professional life but also enhances their overall well-being and satisfaction.

4. Setting an Example for the Organization: CEOs serve as role models for their employees. When CEOs prioritize their own development, it sets a precedent for the entire organization. It communicates the importance of continuous learning, self-improvement, and a growth mindset. This, in turn, inspires and motivates employees to invest in their own development, creating a culture of learning and growth within the organization.
5. Building Resilience and Adaptability: The business landscape is rife with challenges, setbacks, and uncertainties. CEOs must possess the resilience and adaptability to navigate through these situations. By investing in their personal growth, CEOs can develop emotional resilience, mental agility, and the ability to bounce back from failures. They can cultivate a mindset that sees obstacles as opportunities for growth and learning.
6. Driving Innovation and Creativity: CEOs play a crucial role in driving innovation within their organizations. By investing in their personal development, CEOs can nurture their own creativity and innovation skills. They can explore new perspectives, seek inspiration from various sources, and adopt a mindset that encourages experimentation and risk-taking. This, in turn, fosters a culture of innovation within the organization.

7. Strengthening Stakeholder Relationships: CEOs interact with various stakeholders, including employees, customers, investors, and board members. Developing key attributes such as effective communication, empathy, and trustworthiness enables CEOs to build and strengthen these relationships. By investing in their personal growth, CEOs can enhance their ability to connect with stakeholders, understand their needs, and establish mutually beneficial partnerships.
8. Driving Organizational Success: Ultimately, the success of the organization rests on the CEO's shoulders. By investing in their personal development and building on their key attributes, CEOs can improve their decision-making, strategic thinking, and problem-solving abilities. They can foster a high-performance culture, attract and retain top talent, and drive the organization towards its goals and objectives.

Action Plan for CEO's Personal Development:
(In a later chapter, after you've completed these 31 traits, you will have an opportunity with an Action Plan to work on each of these)

- ✓ Self-Assessment: Conduct a thorough assessment of strengths and areas for improvement based on the key attributes. This helps identify the areas that require focus and development.
- ✓ Goal Setting: Set specific, measurable, and realistic goals for personal development. Align these goals with the organization's strategic

objectives to ensure they contribute to overall success.

- ✓ Learning Opportunities: Identify relevant learning opportunities such as workshops, seminars, conferences, and online courses. Engage in continuous learning to enhance knowledge and skills in the identified areas.
- ✓ Executive Coaching: Consider engaging an executive coach or mentor who can provide guidance, support, and feedback on personal development goals. This external perspective can help accelerate growth and provide valuable insights.
- ✓ Networking: Build a strong network of peers, industry leaders, and mentors. Engage in meaningful conversations, seek advice, and learn from the experiences of others.
- ✓ Reflect and Iterate: Regularly reflect on personal growth progress, evaluate the effectiveness of actions taken, and make adjustments as necessary. Continuously iterate the personal development plan to ensure it remains relevant and aligned with evolving needs.
- ✓ Accountability and Measurement: Hold oneself accountable for personal development goals and track progress. Regularly assess the impact of personal growth efforts on leadership effectiveness and organizational outcomes.

Example: A CEO recognizes the need to enhance their strategic thinking. They set a goal to develop this trait by attending a strategic planning workshop, reading books on strategic management, and seeking guidance from a seasoned industry mentor.

They engage in reflection exercises to apply strategic thinking principles to real-life scenarios within the organization. Through this intentional personal development effort, the CEO gains a deeper understanding of the competitive landscape, identifies new growth opportunities, and effectively guides the organization towards strategic goals.

In conclusion, a CEO's personal development and investment in building key attributes are crucial for their own growth, the success of the organization, and the cultivation of a positive work culture. By continuously developing themselves, CEOs can lead with excellence, adapt to change, inspire their teams, drive innovation, and foster long-term success.

Developing the MINDSET of a Successful CEO

To develop a mindset of a successful CEO, leaders can take the following steps:

1. Embrace a Growth Mindset: Adopt a mindset that values continuous learning, growth, and improvement. Embrace challenges, view failures as opportunities for learning, and believe that abilities and intelligence can be developed over time. Example: Instead of being discouraged by setbacks, a leader with a growth mindset would see them as valuable learning experiences, reflect on what went wrong, and adjust their approach accordingly.
2. Cultivate Self-Awareness: Develop a deep understanding of your strengths, weaknesses, values, and biases. Regularly engage in self-reflection and seek feedback from others to gain insights into your leadership style and areas for improvement. Example: A leader may conduct regular self-assessment exercises, such as journaling or seeking feedback from mentors, peers, and direct reports, to gain a better understanding of their leadership strengths and areas that need development.
3. Foster a Strategic Perspective: Develop the ability to think strategically and see the big picture. Cultivate a mindset that considers long-term goals, market trends, and the impact of decisions on the overall organization. Example: A leader may allocate dedicated time for strategic thinking, engage

in scenario planning exercises, or seek input from experts and industry thought leaders to broaden their perspective and make informed strategic decisions.

4. Embody Resilience and Adaptability: Foster a mindset that embraces change, uncertainty, and challenges. Develop resilience to bounce back from setbacks and the ability to adapt quickly to new circumstances and market dynamics. Example: A leader may actively seek out opportunities to step out of their comfort zone, take on new challenges, and encourage their team to embrace change. They may also develop coping mechanisms to manage stress and build their capacity to navigate through ambiguity.
5. Nurture a Customer-Centric Mindset: Develop a deep understanding of customer needs, preferences, and expectations. Cultivate a mindset that prioritizes delivering value and exceptional experiences to customers. Example: A leader may regularly interact with customers, conduct market research, and seek feedback from customers to gain insights into their needs. They may encourage a customer-centric culture within the organization by aligning processes and decision-making with customer requirements.
6. Foster an Innovation Mindset: Cultivate a mindset that values creativity, experimentation, and innovation. Encourage a culture that embraces new ideas, rewards calculated risk-taking, and learns from failures. Example: A leader may establish cross-functional teams, allocate resources for

innovation projects, and create platforms for idea generation and collaboration. They may also celebrate and recognize employees who demonstrate innovative thinking and initiative.

7. Practice Ethical Leadership: Develop a mindset that upholds high ethical standards and values integrity in decision-making and behavior. Lead by example and create a culture of trust and transparency. Example: A leader may establish a code of ethics for the organization, provide ethics training, and encourage open dialogue around ethical dilemmas. They may make decisions based on moral principles and consistently communicate and model ethical behavior.

By following these steps, leaders can develop a mindset that aligns with successful CEOs. This mindset fosters continuous growth, strategic thinking, resilience, customer-centricity, innovation, ethical leadership, and a willingness to adapt to evolving circumstances.

The 31-Day Power Plan: Unlocking Your Success

Today, you will begin this exciting and fruitful journey of exploring the 31 most successful traits of CEO's. You can use these traits in any order you wish by focusing on developing each of these traits and incorporating them into your leadership development plan. You can set specific goals and action steps as recommended, to enhance each trait, aligning them with the organization's strategic objectives. Additionally, you can seek feedback, participate in relevant training programs, and learn from successful leaders who exemplify these traits.

Remember, it is essential for you as a CEO to prioritize and identify the traits that are most relevant to your specific industry, organizational context, and personal development areas. A tailored approach to developing these traits will yield the best results. So let's begin…

Trait 1
Visionary Thinking

Visionary thinking is the ability to anticipate future trends, identify opportunities, and set a clear direction for the organization. This trait is essential for CEOs because it allows them to create a compelling vision that inspires employees, attracts investors, and guides strategic decision-making.

Benefits: A CEO with visionary thinking can anticipate industry trends, identify growth opportunities, and set a clear direction for the organization.
Importance: It helps drive innovation, aligns the organization towards a common purpose, and inspires employees to work towards a shared vision.

Action Plan:

- ✓ Develop a deep understanding of industry trends and emerging technologies.
- ✓ Engage in strategic foresight exercises to envision the future of the organization.
- ✓ Communicate the vision effectively to align and inspire the entire organization.
- ✓ Foster a culture of innovation by encouraging employees to think beyond current boundaries.

e. Monitor and adapt the vision as needed based on market dynamics and feedback.

Example: Steve Jobs, the co-founder of Apple Inc., had a visionary mindset that transformed the technology industry. He envisioned a world where technology seamlessly integrated into people's lives, leading to revolutionary products like the iPhone, iPad, and iTunes. Jobs' vision not only reshaped Apple's future but also influenced the entire consumer electronics industry.

It's your turn now!

What steps will you take to put this trait into your leadership style?

Trait 2
Strategic Mindset

A strategic mindset is crucial for CEOs to navigate complex business environments and make informed decisions that drive long-term growth. It involves analyzing market trends, assessing competitive landscapes, and identifying potential risks and opportunities.

Benefits: CEOs with a strategic mindset can formulate long-term plans, make informed decisions, and effectively allocate resources to achieve organizational goals.
Importance: It ensures the organization stays competitive, adapts to changing market conditions, and maximizes growth opportunities.

Action Plan:

- ✓ Continuously monitor and evaluate the competitive landscape and industry trends.
- ✓ Develop a deep understanding of the organization's strengths, weaknesses, opportunities, and threats (SWOT analysis).
- ✓ Set clear strategic goals and objectives aligned with the vision.
- ✓ Allocate resources effectively to support strategic initiatives.
- ✓ Regularly review and adapt strategies based on feedback and market changes.

Example: Satya Nadella, the CEO of Microsoft, demonstrated a strong strategic mindset by shifting the company's focus towards cloud computing. He recognized the growing demand for cloud-based services and strategically transformed Microsoft to become a leader in the cloud computing industry. This shift has fueled significant revenue growth for the company.

It's your turn now!

What steps will you take to put this trait into your leadership style?

Trait 3
Exceptional Leadership Skills

Exceptional leadership skills are essential for CEOs to inspire, motivate, and align their teams towards achieving shared goals. They create a positive work culture, empower employees, and foster innovation.

Benefits: Effective leadership skills enable CEOs to inspire and motivate employees, build high-performing teams, and foster a positive work culture.
Importance: It improves employee engagement, productivity, and retention, while also influencing organizational performance and success.

Action Plan:

- ✓ Continuously develop self-awareness and emotional intelligence to understand and connect with others.
- ✓ Lead by example and demonstrate integrity, transparency, and ethical behavior.
- ✓ Build strong relationships with employees, stakeholders, and the broader community. d. Empower employees by delegating authority and fostering a culture of ownership and innovation.
- ✓ Invest in leadership development programs to enhance leadership skills.

Example: Jeff Bezos, the founder and former CEO of Amazon, is known for his exceptional leadership skills. He created a customer-focused culture, empowered employees to experiment and innovate, and encouraged a long-term perspective. Bezos' leadership style has been instrumental in Amazon's success as a customer-centric and innovative company.

It’s your turn now!
What steps will you take to put this trait into your leadership style?

Trait 4
Effective Communication

Effective communication is crucial for CEOs to articulate their vision, align stakeholders, and inspire confidence in their leadership. It involves conveying complex ideas clearly, building strong relationships, and resolving conflicts.

Benefits: CEOs with strong communication skills can articulate their vision, build relationships with stakeholders, and foster a culture of transparency and trust.
Importance: It enhances collaboration, ensures alignment across the organization, and facilitates effective decision-making and problem-solving.

Action Plan:

- ✓ Enhance verbal and written communication skills through training and practice.
- ✓ Develop active listening skills to understand the needs and perspectives of others.
- ✓ Use storytelling techniques to engage and inspire stakeholders.
- ✓ Foster open and transparent communication channels within the organization.
- ✓ Adapt communication style to different audiences and contexts.

Example: Indra Nooyi, the former CEO of PepsiCo, demonstrated effective communication skills by effectively conveying the company's strategic vision and values. She communicated the importance of diversity and sustainability and engaged stakeholders in meaningful dialogues, resulting in strengthened relationships and a positive brand image for PepsiCo.

It's your turn now!

What steps will you take to put this trait into your leadership style?

Trait 5
Decisiveness

Decisiveness is crucial for CEOs to make timely and informed decisions in a fast-paced business environment. It involves assessing risks, weighing potential rewards, and taking action to seize opportunities or mitigate risks.

Benefits: CEOs who are decisive can make timely and informed decisions, drive progress, and seize opportunities.
Importance: It accelerates organizational growth, prevents delays, and instills confidence in employees and stakeholders.

Action Plan:

- ✓ Develop a framework for decision-making that considers relevant factors and aligns with organizational values.
- ✓ Seek input and gather necessary information to make informed decisions.
- ✓ Evaluate potential risks and rewards to assess the impact of decisions.
- ✓ Trust your judgment and be willing to take calculated risks.
- ✓ Continuously evaluate and learn from decisions to improve future decision-making.

Example: Tim Cook, the CEO of Apple, has shown decisive leadership by making bold decisions to position Apple as a market leader in the technology industry. Cook made the strategic decision to introduce new product categories, such as the Apple

Watch and AirPods, and expanded into new markets, such as China, which have contributed to Apple's continued success.

It’s your turn now!
What steps will you take to put this trait into your leadership style?

Trait 6
Resilience

Resilience is essential for CEOs to bounce back from setbacks, adapt to change, and lead their organizations through challenging times. It involves the ability to learn from failures, maintain optimism, and persevere in the face of adversity.

Benefits: Resilient CEOs can navigate challenges, bounce back from setbacks, and maintain focus and optimism in the face of adversity.
Importance: It fosters a culture of perseverance, inspires employees to overcome obstacles, and ensures long-term sustainability.

Action Plan:

- ✓ Develop a growth mindset and view failures as learning opportunities.
- ✓ Cultivate a supportive network of mentors, peers, and advisors who can provide guidance and encouragement.
- ✓ Practice self-care and prioritize well-being to maintain resilience.
- ✓ Foster a culture of resilience within the organization by encouraging risk-taking and embracing learning from failures.
- ✓ Seek feedback and reflect on lessons learned from difficult situations.

Example: Mary Barra, the CEO of General Motors, demonstrated resilience by successfully leading the company through a major vehicle recall crisis. She implemented rigorous quality control measures, rebuilt customer trust, and navigated the company through a challenging period. Barra's resilience and leadership were instrumental in General Motors' recovery and ongoing success.

It's your turn now!
What steps will you take to put this trait into your leadership style?

Trait 7
Ethical and Transparent Behavior

Ethical and transparent behavior is crucial for CEOs as it builds trust with stakeholders and establishes a strong corporate reputation. CEOs who uphold high ethical standards inspire loyalty, foster employee engagement, and drive sustainable business practices. Ethical and transparent behavior ensures that CEOs act with integrity, honesty, and fairness in their business dealings. It involves adhering to a strong moral compass, maintaining transparency in decision-making processes, and fostering a culture of ethics throughout the organization.

Benefits: CEOs who prioritize ethics and transparency earn trust and credibility from employees, customers, and stakeholders, leading to strong relationships and long-term success.
Importance: It fosters a positive organizational culture, mitigates risks, and ensures ethical decision-making and responsible corporate governance.

Action Plan:

- ✓ Lead by example: CEOs should demonstrate ethical behavior in their actions, decisions, and interactions.
- ✓ Establish a code of ethics: Develop and communicate a code of ethics that sets clear expectations for ethical behavior across the organization.

- ✓ Provide ethics training: Implement training programs to educate employees on ethical principles and guidelines.
- ✓ Encourage open communication: Create a safe environment for employees to report unethical behavior without fear of retaliation.
- ✓ Regularly assess and reinforce ethical standards: Review and update ethical policies and practices to ensure they remain relevant and effective.

Example: Satya Nadella, the CEO of Microsoft, has emphasized the importance of ethical and transparent behavior. Under his leadership, Microsoft has adopted a strong stance on data privacy and security, ensuring customer trust and compliance with regulatory requirements. Nadella's commitment to ethical behavior has positively influenced the company's culture and reputation.

It's your turn now!
What steps will you take to put this trait into your leadership style?

Trait 8
Financial Acumen

CEOs must possess strong financial acumen to drive profitability, allocate resources effectively, and make informed financial decisions. This trait involves understanding financial statements, market dynamics, and capital allocation strategies. Financial acumen enables CEOs to evaluate the financial health of the organization, identify growth opportunities, and make sound financial decisions. It involves analyzing financial data, understanding key performance indicators, and leveraging financial insights to drive strategic initiatives.

Benefits: CEOs with financial acumen can analyze financial data, make informed business decisions, and drive financial performance and growth.
Importance: It ensures financial stability, effective resource allocation, and maximizes shareholder value.

Action Plan:

- ✓ Enhance financial literacy: CEOs should continuously improve their understanding of financial concepts, including financial statements, cash flow analysis, and financial ratios.
- ✓ Collaborate with financial experts: Seek guidance from CFOs, financial advisors, or mentors to deepen financial acumen and gain different perspectives.

- ✓ Use data-driven decision-making: Utilize financial data and analytics to inform strategic decision-making and resource allocation.
- ✓ Conduct regular financial reviews: Evaluate financial performance, identify areas for improvement, and adjust strategies accordingly.
- ✓ Stay updated on market trends: Keep abreast of industry trends and market conditions that may impact financial outcomes.

Example: Mary Barra, the CEO of General Motors, has demonstrated strong financial acumen by effectively managing the company's financial performance. Under her leadership, General Motors implemented cost-saving initiatives, optimized manufacturing processes, and improved profitability. Barra's financial acumen has played a crucial role in General Motors' financial turnaround.

It's your turn now!
What steps will you take to put this trait into your leadership style?

Trait 9
Customer Focus

Successful CEOs prioritize a customer-centric approach, recognizing the importance of understanding and exceeding customer expectations. This trait involves actively listening to customers, gathering feedback, and aligning products and services with customer needs. Customer focus is essential for CEOs as it drives customer loyalty, enhances brand reputation, and fosters innovation. By understanding customer needs and preferences, CEOs can deliver products and experiences that meet or exceed expectations, leading to long-term success.

Benefits: CEOs who prioritize customer focus can understand customer needs, deliver value, and build loyal customer relationships.
Importance: It drives customer satisfaction, market differentiation, and sustainable revenue growth.

Action Plan:

- ✓ Develop a customer-centric culture: Communicate the importance of customer focus throughout the organization and ensure that it is ingrained in the company's values and behaviors.
- ✓ Gather customer feedback: Establish channels for collecting and analyzing customer feedback, such as surveys, focus groups, or social media listening.
- ✓ Build strong relationships: Interact with customers directly, attend industry events, and

actively engage with key stakeholders to gain insights and build relationships.

- ✓ Leverage data and analytics: Utilize customer data and analytics to identify trends, preferences, and areas for improvement.
- ✓ Continuously innovate: Encourage a culture of innovation and experimentation to develop new products or services that address customer needs.

Example: Jeff Bezos, the founder and former CEO of Amazon, has built a customer-focused culture that has been instrumental in the company's success. By prioritizing customer convenience, fast delivery, and personalized experiences, Amazon has become a leader in e-commerce and set new standards for customer satisfaction.

It's your turn now!

What steps will you take to put this trait into your leadership style?

Trait 10
Innovation and Creativity

CEOs must foster a culture of innovation and creativity to drive business growth and stay ahead of the competition. This trait involves encouraging experimentation, empowering employees to think outside the box, and embracing new ideas. Innovation and creativity enable CEOs to identify new market opportunities, develop unique solutions, and drive continuous improvement. By fostering a culture of innovation, CEOs can harness the collective creativity of their teams and generate groundbreaking ideas.

Benefits: CEOs who foster innovation and creativity can drive product and process improvements, stay ahead of competitors, and adapt to changing market demands.

Importance: It fuels organizational growth, fosters a culture of continuous improvement, and encourages employee engagement and empowerment.

Action Plan:

- ✓ Encourage a growth mindset: Promote a culture that values experimentation, embraces failure as a learning opportunity, and rewards creative thinking.
- ✓ Provide resources for innovation: Allocate dedicated time, budget, and resources for innovation initiatives within the organization.
- ✓ Empower employees: Create platforms for employees to share ideas, collaborate, and contribute to the innovation process.

- ✓ Foster cross-functional collaboration: Encourage teams from different departments to collaborate, exchange ideas, and leverage diverse perspectives.
- ✓ Stay connected to emerging trends: Keep abreast of industry trends, emerging technologies, and customer preferences to identify potential areas for innovation.

Example: Elon Musk, the CEO of Tesla and SpaceX, is renowned for his innovative mindset. Under Musk's leadership, Tesla revolutionized the electric vehicle industry by developing cutting-edge electric cars and advancing battery technology. Musk's creativity and vision have driven innovation in multiple industries, pushing the boundaries of what is possible.

It's your turn now!

What steps will you take to put this trait into your leadership style?

Trait 11
Global Perspective

In today's interconnected world, successful CEOs must have a global perspective, understanding and leveraging opportunities in diverse markets. This trait involves embracing cultural diversity, adapting strategies to local markets, and building global partnerships. A global perspective allows CEOs to expand their businesses beyond local boundaries, tap into new markets, and leverage global talent and resources. Understanding diverse cultures and market dynamics enables CEOs to develop strategies that resonate with international audiences.

Benefits: CEOs with a global perspective can identify international market opportunities, navigate cultural complexities, and develop effective global strategies.
Importance: It facilitates global expansion, diversifies revenue streams, and enhances competitiveness in a globalized economy.

Action Plan:

- ✓ Develop cultural intelligence: Invest in learning about different cultures, customs, and business practices to facilitate effective communication and relationship-building.
- ✓ Expand international networks: Actively engage in global networks, industry associations, and conferences to build relationships and gain insights into international markets.

- ✓ Customize strategies for local markets: Adapt business strategies, products, and marketing approaches to suit the preferences and needs of specific target markets.
- ✓ Establish local partnerships: Forge strategic alliances and partnerships with local companies or distributors to access market knowledge and distribution channels.
- ✓ Embrace diversity and inclusion: Foster an inclusive work environment that values diverse perspectives and encourages collaboration across cultures.

Example: Ajay Banga, the former CEO of Mastercard, is known for his global perspective. Under his leadership, Mastercard expanded its presence in emerging markets and drove financial inclusion initiatives worldwide. Banga's global perspective enabled Mastercard to tailor its offerings to diverse markets and capture new growth opportunities.

It's your turn now!

What steps will you take to put this trait into your leadership style?

Trait 12
Adaptability

CEOs must be adaptable and open to change to thrive in dynamic business environments. This trait involves being receptive to new ideas, adjusting strategies as needed, and fostering a culture of continuous learning. Adaptability enables CEOs to navigate uncertainties, embrace emerging technologies, and seize new opportunities. By being open to change, CEOs can lead their organizations through transformations and ensure long-term success.

Benefits: CEOs who are adaptable can respond to market changes, embrace new technologies, and lead organizational transformations.

Importance: It ensures organizational agility, facilitates innovation, and enables the organization to stay relevant and resilient in a dynamic business environment.

Action Plan:

- ✓ Embrace a growth mindset: Foster a culture that encourages learning, experimentation, and continuous improvement.
- ✓ Encourage feedback and diverse perspectives: Create channels for employees to provide feedback, share ideas, and contribute to decision-making processes.
- ✓ Stay updated on industry trends: Continuously monitor market trends, technological advancements, and customer behaviors to identify potential disruptions or opportunities.

d. Foster agility in decision-making: Encourage rapid decision-making processes that allow for flexibility and adaptation to changing circumstances.

- ✓ Invest in personal and professional development: Continuously develop skills, seek learning opportunities, and encourage employees to do the same.

Example: Satya Nadella, the CEO of Microsoft, has demonstrated adaptability by leading the company through a successful transformation from a traditional software-focused company to a cloud computing and services company. Nadella's ability to adapt to changing market dynamics and embrace new technologies has been instrumental in Microsoft's continued growth.

It's your turn now!

What steps will you take to put this trait into your leadership style?

Trait 13
Emotional Intelligence

Emotional intelligence refers to the ability to recognize, understand, and manage one's own emotions and the emotions of others. It is essential for CEOs as it enables them to build strong relationships, lead with empathy, and navigate complex interpersonal dynamics effectively. Emotional intelligence allows CEOs to foster a positive work environment, resolve conflicts, and inspire trust among employees, stakeholders, and customers. By understanding and managing emotions, CEOs can make more informed decisions and respond appropriately to various situations.

Benefits: CEOs with high emotional intelligence can understand and manage their own emotions, build strong relationships, and effectively lead and motivate others.
Importance: It improves communication, teamwork, and employee satisfaction, and enhances overall leadership effectiveness.

Action Plan:

- ✓ Develop self-awareness: Reflect on personal strengths, weaknesses, and emotional triggers. Seek feedback from trusted colleagues or mentors.
- ✓ Enhance empathy: Put yourself in others' shoes and actively listen to their perspectives. Show genuine care and understanding.
- ✓ Practice emotional regulation: Develop strategies to manage stress, maintain

composure, and handle challenging situations with emotional intelligence.

- ✓ Build strong relationships: Foster open communication, establish rapport, and create a supportive work culture that values emotional well-being.
- ✓ Invest in emotional intelligence training: Participate in workshops or coaching sessions focused on developing emotional intelligence skills.

Example: Satya Nadella, the CEO of Microsoft, is known for his high emotional intelligence. He has transformed Microsoft's culture by emphasizing empathy, fostering a collaborative work environment, and encouraging open dialogue. Nadella's emotional intelligence has positively influenced employee morale and engagement, leading to improved productivity and innovation.

It's your turn now!
What steps will you take to put this trait into your leadership style?

Trait 14
Risk-Taking

CEOs need to be comfortable taking calculated risks to drive innovation, seize opportunities, and stay ahead in competitive markets. Risk-taking involves making decisions in the face of uncertainty and being willing to accept the potential consequences. Risk-taking is essential for CEOs as it allows them to explore new markets, develop disruptive strategies, and lead their organizations through change. By embracing calculated risks, CEOs can inspire their teams to be innovative and agile, leading to growth and differentiation.

Benefits: CEOs who are willing to take calculated risks can seize growth opportunities, foster innovation, and gain a competitive advantage.
Importance: It encourages a culture of innovation, drives business growth, and enables the organization to adapt and evolve.

Action Plan:

- ✓ Foster a culture of experimentation: Encourage employees to think outside the box, share ideas, and pursue innovative projects.
- ✓ Assess risks and rewards: Conduct thorough analysis and evaluation of potential risks, weighing them against potential rewards.
- ✓ Develop contingency plans: Prepare backup strategies to mitigate potential risks and respond effectively to unexpected challenges.

- ✓ Encourage learning from failures: Create an environment where failures are seen as learning opportunities, and encourage employees to share and reflect on their experiences.
- ✓ Lead by example: Demonstrate a willingness to take calculated risks, communicate the rationale behind decisions, and learn from outcomes.

Example: Reed Hastings, the CEO of Netflix, has shown a propensity for risk-taking. Under his leadership, Netflix transitioned from a DVD-by-mail service to a streaming platform, disrupting the traditional entertainment industry. By taking risks and investing in original content, Hastings positioned Netflix as a global leader in the streaming space.

It's your turn now!

What steps will you take to put this trait into your leadership style?

Trait 15
Learning Agility

Learning agility refers to the ability to rapidly learn and adapt in dynamic environments. It involves being open to new ideas, seeking feedback, and continuously developing new skills and knowledge. In rapidly changing markets, CEOs need to be agile learners to stay ahead of industry trends, embrace new technologies, and drive innovation. Learning agility allows CEOs to make informed decisions, lead with flexibility, and inspire a culture of continuous improvement.

Benefits: CEOs with learning agility can quickly acquire new knowledge and skills, adapt to new situations, and drive personal and organizational growth.

Importance: It facilitates continuous improvement, enables leaders to stay ahead of industry trends, and fosters a culture of learning and development.

Action Plan:

- ✓ Foster a growth mindset: Encourage curiosity, a hunger for knowledge, and a willingness to learn from experiences.
- ✓ Embrace diverse learning opportunities: Attend conferences, participate in industry events, and engage in networking to broaden perspectives and gain new insights.
- ✓ Seek feedback: Actively seek input from employees, peers, and mentors to identify areas for improvement and growth.

- ✓ Develop learning plans: Set personal development goals, prioritize learning activities, and allocate time for continuous learning.
- ✓ Encourage organizational learning: Foster a learning culture by providing training programs, knowledge-sharing platforms, and opportunities for cross-functional collaboration.

Example: Ginni Rometty, the former CEO of IBM, prioritized learning agility during her tenure. She led IBM's transformation into a cognitive solutions and cloud platform company by investing in emerging technologies like artificial intelligence and blockchain. Rometty's emphasis on learning and adaptation enabled IBM to remain relevant and competitive in the rapidly evolving technology landscape.

It's your turn now!

What steps will you take to put this trait into your leadership style?

Trait 16
Empathy

Empathy refers to the ability to understand and share the feelings of others. It allows CEOs to connect with their teams, create a supportive work culture, and make decisions that consider the well-being of employees and stakeholders. Empathy is essential for CEOs as it builds trust, strengthens relationships, and enhances employee engagement and satisfaction. By demonstrating empathy, CEOs can create a positive work environment that fosters collaboration, creativity, and loyalty.

Benefits: CEOs who demonstrate empathy can connect with their employees, understand their needs, and create a supportive work environment.
Importance: It enhances employee morale, fosters loyalty and commitment, and drives employee engagement and well-being.

Action Plan:

- ✓ Practice active listening: Pay attention to verbal and non-verbal cues, demonstrate genuine interest, and provide a safe space for open communication.
- ✓ Seek diverse perspectives: Encourage diversity of thought and create opportunities for employees to share their experiences and viewpoints.
- ✓ Lead with compassion: Show understanding and support during challenging times, provide resources for personal well-being, and promote work-life balance.

- ✓ Incorporate empathy in decision-making: Consider the impact of decisions on individuals and teams, and communicate decisions with empathy and transparency.
- ✓ Provide empathy training: Offer workshops or training sessions to develop empathy skills and foster a culture of compassion within the organization.

Example: Hubert Joly, the former CEO of Best Buy, prioritized empathy as part of the company's turnaround strategy. He implemented the "Renew Blue" transformation plan, which focused on creating a customer-centric culture and empowering employees to deliver exceptional customer experiences. Joly's empathetic leadership style created a supportive and customer-focused environment, leading to improved customer satisfaction and business results.

It's your turn now!
What steps will you take to put this trait into your leadership style?

Trait 17
Authenticity

Authenticity refers to being true to oneself, displaying genuine character, and leading with integrity. Authentic CEOs are transparent, consistent, and inspire trust among employees, stakeholders, and customers. Authenticity is essential for CEOs as it builds credibility, fosters trust, and creates a positive work environment. By leading with authenticity, CEOs can establish strong relationships, motivate their teams, and inspire loyalty.

Benefits: CEOs who are authentic inspire trust, build credibility, and create an environment where employees feel safe to be their true selves.
Importance: It fosters genuine connections, encourages open communication, and strengthens relationships with employees, customers, and stakeholders.

Action Plan:

- ✓ Reflect on personal values and purpose: Identify core values and align actions with those values. Understand personal strengths, weaknesses, and areas for growth.
- ✓ Communicate with transparency: Share information openly, admit mistakes, and provide honest feedback to build trust and credibility.
- ✓ Demonstrate consistency: Align words with actions, maintain a consistent leadership style, and uphold ethical standards in all interactions.

- ✓ Encourage authenticity throughout the organization: Create an environment that values individuality, diverse perspectives, and encourages employees to bring their whole selves to work.
- ✓ Seek feedback on authenticity: Regularly solicit feedback from employees, peers, and mentors to ensure alignment between perception and intended authenticity.

Example: Howard Schultz, the former CEO of Starbucks, exemplified authenticity in his leadership. He led with a strong sense of purpose, prioritizing the company's values and social responsibility. Schultz's authenticity and commitment to his vision of creating a "third place" between work and home contributed to Starbucks' success and its reputation as a socially conscious brand.

It's your turn now!

What steps will you take to put this trait into your leadership style?

Trait 18
Problem-Solving

Problem-solving refers to the ability to analyze complex situations, identify challenges, and develop effective solutions. CEOs who excel in problem-solving can navigate obstacles, make informed decisions, and drive organizational success. Problem-solving is essential for CEOs as they are faced with numerous challenges in their roles. CEOs must be able to approach problems systematically, gather relevant information, and generate innovative solutions that address the root causes of issues.

Benefits: CEOs who excel in problem-solving can identify and resolve complex issues, drive innovation, and find creative solutions.
Importance: It enables effective decision-making, enhances efficiency, and ensures obstacles are overcome to achieve organizational objectives.

Action Plan:

- ✓ Develop analytical thinking skills: Enhance critical thinking abilities, including data analysis, logical reasoning, and pattern recognition.
- ✓ Encourage collaboration: Foster a collaborative environment that encourages cross-functional problem-solving and collective intelligence.
- ✓ Use structured problem-solving frameworks: Adopt frameworks such as root cause analysis, SWOT analysis, or design thinking to approach complex problems.

- ✓ Embrace creativity and innovation: Encourage employees to think outside the box, explore multiple solutions, and challenge traditional thinking.
- ✓ Continuously evaluate and refine solutions: Monitor the effectiveness of implemented solutions, gather feedback, and iterate as necessary.

Example: Tim Cook, the CEO of Apple, has demonstrated exceptional problem-solving skills. Cook successfully led Apple through supply chain challenges, product development complexities, and market competition. His analytical thinking and ability to identify and address critical issues have played a significant role in Apple's ongoing success.

It's your turn now!

What steps will you take to put this trait into your leadership style?

Trait 19
Collaboration

Collaboration refers to the ability to work effectively with others, leveraging their diverse skills and perspectives to achieve shared goals. It involves fostering teamwork, promoting open communication, and creating a culture of collaboration within the organization. Collaboration is essential for CEOs as it enables them to harness the collective intelligence of their teams, drive innovation, and achieve superior results. By fostering collaboration, CEOs can break down silos, encourage knowledge sharing, and create an environment where ideas and expertise are freely exchanged.

Benefits: CEOs who promote collaboration can harness the collective intelligence of their teams, drive innovation, and foster a sense of ownership and engagement.
Importance: It enhances problem-solving, encourages diverse perspectives, and strengthens teamwork and cooperation.

Action Plan:

- ✓ Promote a collaborative culture: Communicate the importance of collaboration, set expectations, and lead by example by collaborating with others.
- ✓ Establish cross-functional teams: Create opportunities for employees from different departments to work together on projects, encouraging diverse perspectives and interdisciplinary collaboration.

- ✓ Provide collaborative tools and platforms: Implement technologies that facilitate communication, file sharing, and collaborative project management.
- ✓ Recognize and reward collaboration: Acknowledge and appreciate individuals and teams who demonstrate effective collaboration and achieve collective goals.
- ✓ Encourage continuous learning and development: Offer training programs on effective collaboration, conflict resolution, and team dynamics.

Example: Sundar Pichai, the CEO of Google, encourages a collaborative work environment where employees are given time to collaborate on innovative projects. Through initiatives like "20% time," employees are encouraged to spend a portion of their work time on projects of personal interest, fostering cross-functional collaboration and driving innovation within the company.

It’s your turn now!
What steps will you take to put this trait into your leadership style?

Trait 20
Accountability

Accountability refers to taking responsibility for one's actions and outcomes. It involves setting clear expectations, holding oneself and others accountable, and ensuring commitments are fulfilled. Accountability is essential for CEOs as it fosters trust, builds credibility, and ensures that goals and objectives are met. By promoting accountability, CEOs create a culture of ownership and drive performance excellence throughout the organization.

Benefits: CEOs who prioritize accountability create a culture of responsibility, drive performance, and ensure the achievement of goals and targets.

Importance: It promotes a sense of ownership, instills discipline, and fosters a high-performance culture.

Action Plan:

- ✓ Set clear expectations: Define roles, responsibilities, and performance targets for individuals and teams, ensuring alignment with organizational goals.
- ✓ Establish metrics and milestones: Implement key performance indicators (KPIs) and milestones to track progress and hold individuals accountable for their deliverables.
- ✓ Provide regular feedback: Conduct performance evaluations and provide constructive feedback to support growth and improvement.

- ✓ Lead by example: Demonstrate personal accountability by following through on commitments, admitting mistakes, and taking corrective action when necessary.
- ✓ Foster a culture of learning from failures: Encourage individuals to learn from their mistakes, share lessons learned, and apply those learnings to future endeavors.

Example: Mary Barra, the CEO of General Motors, prioritizes accountability within the organization. She implemented a system that holds leaders accountable for product quality and safety, emphasizing the importance of taking responsibility for delivering safe and reliable vehicles to customers.

It's your turn now!

What steps will you take to put this trait into your leadership style?

Trait 21
Integrity

Integrity refers to the adherence to ethical principles, honesty, and moral soundness. It involves acting with transparency, upholding strong ethical values, and being consistent in word and deed. Integrity is essential for CEOs as it builds trust, fosters credibility, and establishes a strong ethical foundation for the organization. CEOs with integrity inspire loyalty among employees, gain the trust of stakeholders, and create a positive reputation for the company.

Benefits: CEOs who demonstrate integrity earn trust and credibility, enhance reputation, and build strong relationships with stakeholders.
Importance: It establishes a foundation of ethical behavior, reinforces corporate values, and sets the tone for the organization's culture.

Action Plan:

- ✓ Define and communicate ethical standards: Establish a code of ethics that outlines the organization's core values and ethical principles.
- ✓ Lead by example: Demonstrate integrity in all aspects of decision-making, communication, and behavior, setting the standard for ethical conduct.
- ✓ Encourage ethical decision-making: Foster an open culture where employees feel comfortable raising ethical concerns and

provide guidance on ethical decision-making processes.

- ✓ Implement controls and checks: Establish mechanisms to ensure compliance with ethical standards, such as regular audits, whistleblower policies, and ethics training.
- ✓ Recognize and reward ethical behavior: Celebrate individuals who demonstrate integrity and ethical conduct, reinforcing the importance of ethical behavior within the organization.

Example: Satya Nadella, the CEO of Microsoft, has prioritized integrity within the company. Under his leadership, Microsoft has taken significant steps to strengthen its commitment to ethical practices, including enhanced privacy protections and increased transparency in data handling.

It's your turn now!

What steps will you take to put this trait into your leadership style?

Trait 22
Continuous Improvement

Continuous improvement refers to the ongoing effort to enhance processes, systems, and performance. It involves seeking opportunities for growth, encouraging innovation, and driving organizational excellence. Continuous improvement is essential for CEOs as it enables organizations to adapt to changing market dynamics, drive innovation, and maintain a competitive edge. By fostering a culture of continuous improvement, CEOs promote innovation, efficiency, and effectiveness throughout the organization.

Benefits: CEOs who foster a culture of continuous improvement drive operational excellence, adapt to changing market conditions, and stay ahead of competitors.

Importance: It promotes innovation, increases efficiency and productivity, and ensures long-term sustainability and growth.

Action Plan:

- ✓ Foster a growth mindset: Encourage employees to embrace learning, view failures as opportunities for improvement, and seek innovative solutions.
- ✓ Establish feedback loops: Regularly gather feedback from employees, customers, and stakeholders to identify areas for improvement and innovation.
- ✓ Encourage knowledge sharing: Create platforms and processes for employees to

share best practices, lessons learned, and innovative ideas.

- ✓ Invest in technology and automation: Continuously evaluate and invest in technologies that streamline processes, enhance productivity, and enable data-driven decision-making.
- ✓ Empower employees to drive improvement: Encourage and support employees in taking ownership of process improvement initiatives and provide resources for training and development.

Example: Jeff Bezos, the founder and former CEO of Amazon, is known for his relentless pursuit of continuous improvement. Under his leadership, Amazon has continuously evolved its operations, introducing innovations such as one-click purchasing, personalized recommendations, and same-day delivery.

It's your turn now!

What steps will you take to put this trait into your leadership style?

Trait 23
Team Building

Team building refers to the ability to assemble and develop high-performing teams, foster collaboration, and create an environment where individuals can thrive and contribute their best work. Team building is essential for CEOs as it enables the organization to leverage the collective talents and skills of its workforce. CEOs who excel in team building can create cohesive and high-performing teams that drive innovation, achieve goals, and adapt to change.

Benefits: CEOs who prioritize team building can attract top talent, foster collaboration and synergy, and create high-performing teams.
Importance: It enhances employee engagement, facilitates knowledge sharing, and drives organizational success through effective teamwork.

Action Plan:

- ✓ Define team roles and goals: Clearly define team roles, responsibilities, and objectives to align individual contributions with the overall team's success.
- ✓ Foster a culture of trust and respect: Create an environment where individuals feel safe to express their ideas, share feedback, and collaborate.
- ✓ Encourage diversity and inclusion: Embrace diversity in all its forms and create opportunities for individuals with different backgrounds and perspectives to contribute to the team.

- ✓ Provide professional development opportunities: Invest in training and development programs to enhance team members' skills, foster career growth, and promote collaboration.
- ✓ Celebrate team achievements: Recognize and reward team achievements to reinforce a culture of collaboration and motivate individuals to work together towards common goals.

Example: Indra Nooyi, the former CEO of PepsiCo, emphasized team building throughout her tenure. She encouraged collaboration across departments and implemented programs that brought together diverse teams to work on innovation and sustainability initiatives.

It’s your turn now!

What steps will you take to put this trait into your leadership style?

Trait 24
Flexibility

Flexibility refers to the ability to adapt and respond to changing circumstances, embrace new ideas, and adjust strategies when necessary. It involves being open-minded, agile, and willing to challenge the status quo. Flexibility is essential for CEOs as it enables them to navigate uncertainty, capitalize on emerging opportunities, and lead their organizations through change. CEOs who are flexible can make timely adjustments to strategies, processes, and resources to drive sustainable growth.

Benefits: CEOs who demonstrate flexibility can adapt to changing circumstances, seize new opportunities, and navigate uncertain business environments.
Importance: It enables agility, facilitates innovation, and ensures the organization can respond effectively to market dynamics and customer needs.

Action Plan:

- ✓ Embrace a growth mindset: Encourage employees to embrace change, view challenges as opportunities, and be open to new ideas and perspectives.
- ✓ Foster a culture of agility: Promote an environment where employees feel empowered to experiment, take calculated risks, and adapt to changing circumstances. c. Foster cross-functional collaboration: Break down silos and encourage collaboration across departments, enabling the organization

to respond quickly and effectively to new challenges.

- ✓ Develop scenario planning capabilities: Anticipate potential scenarios and develop contingency plans to ensure flexibility in responding to unexpected events.
- ✓ Lead with transparency and communication: Keep employees informed about changes, provide context, and ensure clear communication channels to minimize resistance and foster support for new initiatives.

Example: Elon Musk, the CEO of Tesla and SpaceX, is known for his flexibility and ability to adapt to changing market conditions. He has led Tesla through significant transformations, adjusting strategies and products based on market demands and technological advancements.

It's your turn now!

What steps will you take to put this trait into your leadership style?

Trait 25
Patience

Patience refers to the ability to remain calm and composed in the face of challenges, setbacks, or delays. It involves understanding that achieving long-term success requires time and perseverance. Patience is essential for CEOs as they navigate complex business landscapes, make strategic decisions, and lead their organizations through various stages of growth. By cultivating patience, CEOs can avoid making hasty decisions, maintain focus on long-term goals, and inspire confidence in their leadership.

Benefits: CEOs who practice patience can navigate through challenges and setbacks with a calm and composed demeanor. Patience allows CEOs to make thoughtful decisions, build strong relationships, and maintain a long-term perspective.

Importance: Patience is essential for CEOs as it enables them to handle complex situations, such as organizational changes or market fluctuations, with composure. It prevents hasty decision-making, promotes thorough analysis, and allows for the evaluation of various options before taking action.

Action Plan:

- ✓ Develop emotional intelligence: Build self-awareness and self-regulation to manage emotions effectively, especially during high-pressure situations.
- ✓ Set realistic expectations: Understand that meaningful progress takes time and

communicate this perspective to stakeholders, employees, and investors.

- ✓ Foster a supportive work environment: Encourage a culture that recognizes the importance of patience, values learning from failures, and celebrates long-term achievements.
- ✓ Practice mindfulness and stress management techniques: Engage in practices such as meditation, deep breathing, or exercise to promote patience and resilience.
- ✓ Seek perspective from mentors and advisors: Surround yourself with experienced professionals who can provide guidance and support during challenging times.

Example: Jeff Weiner, the former CEO of LinkedIn, demonstrated patience when he led the company through its early years of growth. He focused on building a strong user base and nurturing relationships with key stakeholders, despite facing challenges and market uncertainties. His patience paid off as LinkedIn became a successful global platform.

It's your turn now!

What steps will you take to put this trait into your leadership style?

Trait 26
Cultural Competence

Cultural competence refers to the ability to understand and navigate diverse cultural norms, values, and practices. It involves being open-minded, respectful, and inclusive in working with individuals from different backgrounds. Cultural competence is essential for CEOs as they lead diverse teams, operate in global markets, and foster inclusive work environments. By embracing cultural competence, CEOs can harness the full potential of diverse perspectives, effectively collaborate across cultures, and create a culture of belonging.

Benefits: CEOs with cultural competence can effectively engage with diverse employees, customers, and partners, leading to better understanding and stronger relationships.
Importance: It enhances cross-cultural collaboration, reduces cultural misunderstandings, and drives success in global markets.

Action Plan:

- ✓ Develop cultural awareness: Invest time in learning about different cultures, their values, communication styles, and business practices.
- ✓ Promote diversity and inclusion: Establish policies and practices that promote diversity in hiring, provide equal opportunities, and create a safe and inclusive work environment.
- ✓ Encourage cultural sensitivity training: Offer training programs that educate employees on

cultural differences, promote empathy, and enhance cross-cultural communication skills.

- ✓ Foster cross-cultural collaboration: Create opportunities for employees from different cultural backgrounds to work together on projects, encouraging the exchange of ideas and diverse viewpoints.
- ✓ Seek diverse perspectives in decision-making: Actively solicit input from individuals with diverse cultural backgrounds to ensure decisions consider a broad range of perspectives.

Example: Satya Nadella, the CEO of Microsoft, has prioritized cultural competence within the company. Under his leadership, Microsoft has invested in diversity and inclusion initiatives, established employee resource groups, and fostered a culture that celebrates diversity as a source of strength and innovation.

It's your turn now!

What steps will you take to put this trait into your leadership style?

Trait 27
Strategic Networking

Strategic networking refers to the intentional cultivation of relationships with individuals who can provide support, guidance, and opportunities for professional growth. It involves building a network of trusted contacts within and outside the organization. Strategic networking is essential for CEOs as it allows them to access valuable insights, opportunities for collaboration, and industry knowledge. By building a strong network, CEOs can expand their influence, gain access to resources, and enhance their leadership effectiveness.

Benefits: CEOs who engage in strategic networking build valuable relationships with key industry players, potential partners, and thought leaders. This allows them to access new opportunities, stay informed about industry trends, and gain insights and knowledge from experienced professionals.

Importance: Strategic networking expands the CEO's sphere of influence, facilitates collaboration and knowledge-sharing, and opens doors to potential partnerships, investments, and growth opportunities.

Action Plan:

- ✓ Identify networking goals: Define specific objectives for networking, such as seeking mentorship, exploring partnerships, or gaining industry insights.
- ✓ Attend industry events and conferences: Actively participate in relevant conferences, seminars, and industry forums to meet like-

minded professionals and thought leaders. c. Seek out mentorship opportunities: Establish relationships with experienced individuals who can provide guidance, advice, and support.

- ✓ Leverage online platforms: Utilize social media and professional networking platforms to connect with industry experts and engage in meaningful discussions.
- ✓ Offer support and value to others: Be proactive in helping others, offering assistance, and sharing knowledge and expertise without expecting immediate returns.

Example: Sheryl Sandberg, the COO of Facebook, is known for her strategic networking skills. She has built a vast network of influential professionals, mentors, and advisors, which has helped her navigate career challenges, access new opportunities, and gain insights from diverse perspectives.

It's your turn now!
What steps will you take to put this trait into your leadership style?

Trait 28
Focus on Results

Focus on results refers to the ability to set clear goals, prioritize tasks, and drive outcomes. It involves staying focused on key objectives and ensuring that actions align with desired results. Focus on results is essential for CEOs as it ensures efficient resource allocation, drives accountability, and facilitates progress towards strategic goals. By maintaining a results-oriented mindset, CEOs can inspire a culture of high performance and achievement.

Benefits: CEOs who prioritize a focus on results ensure that the organization remains aligned with its goals and objectives. By setting clear expectations, tracking progress, and holding themselves and their teams accountable, CEOs can drive performance, achieve targets, and enhance overall organizational success.

Importance: A focus on results promotes a culture of performance, drives efficiency, and enables the organization to deliver value to its stakeholders

Action Plan:

- ✓ Set SMART goals: Define specific, measurable, attainable, relevant, and time-bound goals that align with the organization's strategic objectives.
- ✓ Develop action plans: Break down goals into actionable steps, assign responsibilities, and establish timelines to track progress.
- ✓ Monitor key performance indicators (KPIs): Identify relevant metrics and establish a

system to regularly monitor and evaluate performance against set targets.

- ✓ Foster accountability: Create a culture where individuals take ownership of their tasks, track their progress, and report on results.
- ✓ Recognize and reward achievement: Celebrate successes, acknowledge individuals and teams that meet or exceed expectations, and provide incentives to drive motivation.

Example: Elon Musk, the CEO of Tesla and SpaceX, is known for his relentless focus on results. He sets ambitious goals for his companies and drives the organizations towards achieving them. Under his leadership, Tesla has successfully disrupted the automotive industry with its electric vehicles and sustainable energy solutions.

It's your turn now!

What steps will you take to put this trait into your leadership style?

Trait 29
Conflict Resolution

Conflict resolution refers to the ability to manage and resolve conflicts constructively, promoting collaboration and maintaining positive relationships. It involves effective communication, active listening, and finding mutually beneficial solutions. Conflict resolution is essential for CEOs as they navigate complex organizational dynamics, diverse perspectives, and conflicting interests. By demonstrating effective conflict resolution skills, CEOs can minimize disruptions, foster a positive work environment, and promote collaboration and innovation.

Benefits: CEOs who excel in conflict resolution can effectively manage disagreements and disputes, leading to improved collaboration, teamwork, and employee satisfaction. By addressing conflicts promptly and constructively, CEOs can maintain a positive work environment and foster healthy relationships within the organization.

Importance: Conflict resolution reduces workplace tension, enhances productivity, and ensures that conflicts do not escalate and negatively impact organizational performance.

Action Plan:

- ✓ Promote open communication: Encourage employees to express their concerns, provide feedback, and engage in constructive dialogue.

- ✓ Actively listen to all parties: Create a safe space for individuals to share their viewpoints, actively listen without judgment, and demonstrate empathy.
- ✓ Seek common ground: Facilitate discussions to identify shared goals and interests, and encourage parties to focus on finding mutually beneficial solutions.
- ✓ Mediate and facilitate resolution: When conflicts arise, intervene as a neutral party, mediate discussions, and help parties find common ground.
- ✓ Provide conflict resolution training: Offer workshops or training programs that equip employees with conflict resolution skills and strategies.

Example: Mary Barra, the CEO of General Motors, successfully navigated conflicts and facilitated a resolution during the 2014 ignition switch crisis. She took swift action to address the issue, established an independent compensation fund for victims, and worked towards rebuilding trust with stakeholders.

It's your turn now!

What steps will you take to put this trait into your leadership style?

Trait 30
Time Management

Time management refers to the ability to prioritize tasks, allocate time effectively, and optimize productivity. It involves setting goals, planning, and using tools and strategies to maximize efficiency. Time management is essential for CEOs as they face competing priorities, deadlines, and a myriad of responsibilities. By effectively managing their time, CEOs can enhance productivity, minimize stress, and allocate resources efficiently.

Benefits: CEOs who practice effective time management optimize their productivity, prioritize tasks, and make the most of their available time. By focusing on high-value activities and delegating tasks appropriately, CEOs can achieve better work-life balance, reduce stress, and increase overall effectiveness.

Importance: Time management maximizes productivity, enables CEOs to stay organized and meet deadlines, and ensures that critical tasks and strategic priorities are given the necessary attention.

Action Plan:

- ✓ Set clear priorities: Identify high-value tasks that align with strategic objectives and focus on those first.
- ✓ Delegate tasks: Delegate responsibilities to competent team members, empowering them to take ownership and contribute to the organization's success.

- ✓ Establish routines and schedules: Develop a structured routine, allocate time blocks for specific activities, and avoid multitasking.
- ✓ Use technology and tools: Leverage productivity apps, calendar tools, and project management software to manage tasks, deadlines, and schedules.
- ✓ Continuously evaluate and adjust: Regularly assess time management practices, identify inefficiencies, and make necessary adjustments to optimize productivity.

Example: Tim Cook, the CEO of Apple, is known for his exceptional time management skills. He maintains a disciplined routine, starts his day early, and allocates focused time for strategic decision-making, product development, and meetings, allowing him to effectively lead a global technology company.

It's your turn now!
What steps will you take to put this trait into your leadership style?

Trait 31
Self-Reflection

Self-reflection refers to the practice of introspection, self-assessment, and self-awareness. It involves regularly examining one's thoughts, emotions, and actions to gain insights and drive personal growth. Self-reflection is essential for CEOs as it enables them to understand their strengths, weaknesses, and areas for improvement. By practicing self-reflection, CEOs can enhance their self-awareness, make better decisions, and continuously evolve as leaders.

Benefits: CEOs who engage in self-reflection gain valuable insights into their strengths, weaknesses, and areas for improvement. By taking time for introspection, CEOs can enhance their self-awareness, make better decisions, and continuously evolve as leaders.

Importance: Self-reflection fosters personal growth, drives continuous improvement, and enables CEOs to identify and address blind spots. It promotes learning from past experiences and facilitates professional development.

Action Plan:

a. Allocate time for self-reflection: Set aside dedicated time on a regular basis for introspection and self-assessment.

b. Journaling: Maintain a journal to record thoughts, insights, and reflections on experiences, challenges, and successes.

c. Seek feedback from others: Solicit feedback from colleagues, mentors, and trusted advisors to gain different perspectives and identify blind spots.
d. Engage in mindfulness practices: Practice mindfulness meditation or other techniques to enhance self-awareness, clarity, and focus.
e. Develop a personal development plan: Set goals for personal growth, identify specific actions to achieve those goals, and track progress over time.

Example: Satya Nadella, the CEO of Microsoft, emphasizes the importance of self-reflection and mindfulness. He attributes his leadership growth to self-reflection practices and regularly takes time to reflect on his decisions, assess their impact, and learn from experiences.

It's your turn now!
What steps will you take to put this trait into your leadership style?

Bonus and a Very Important Trait: Etiquette & Grooming

Benefits:

- ✓ Professional Image: Etiquette and grooming contribute to projecting a professional image as a CEO. It instills confidence in employees, stakeholders, and clients, creating a positive perception of leadership competence.
- ✓ Respectful Interactions: Etiquette promotes respectful and courteous interactions, fostering a harmonious work environment. It enhances relationships with employees, clients, and business partners, leading to better collaboration and trust.
- ✓ Brand Ambassadorship: As a CEO, you are a representative of your organization. Etiquette and grooming reflect the values and culture of the company, influencing how it is perceived by external stakeholders.
- ✓ Personal Presence: Attention to grooming enhances personal presence and charisma. It conveys a level of professionalism, attention to detail, and self-respect, making a lasting impression on others.

Importance:

- ✓ Professionalism: Etiquette and grooming are critical for projecting professionalism as a CEO. They contribute to a polished and credible image, which is essential for establishing authority and inspiring confidence.

- ✓ Relationship Building: Etiquette fosters positive relationships with employees, clients, and stakeholders. It demonstrates respect, courtesy, and attentiveness, making others feel valued and appreciated.
- ✓ Leadership Example: As a leader, your behavior sets the standard for the organization. Demonstrating proper etiquette and grooming practices creates a culture of professionalism and excellence.
- ✓ Reputation Management: Etiquette and grooming play a role in managing your personal and professional reputation. Consistently presenting yourself in a polished manner enhances your credibility and can positively impact your career trajectory.

Action Plan:

- ✓ Personal Grooming: Maintain good personal hygiene, dress appropriately for different occasions, and pay attention to grooming details such as hairstyle, grooming, and overall appearance.
- ✓ Professional Etiquette: Familiarize yourself with professional etiquette norms in various business settings. This includes understanding proper greetings, dining etiquette, respectful communication, and maintaining professional boundaries.
- ✓ Cultural Sensitivity: Develop cultural competence by understanding and respecting diverse cultural practices and norms, especially in an increasingly globalized business environment.

- ✓ Continuous Learning: Invest time in personal development to enhance your knowledge of etiquette and grooming. Attend workshops, read books, or seek guidance from experts in the field to stay updated on best practices.
- ✓ Lead by Example: Demonstrate etiquette and grooming in your interactions with employees and stakeholders. Model respectful behavior, effective communication, and proper professional appearance, inspiring others to follow suit.

Example: A CEO attends a high-profile industry conference where they have the opportunity to interact with key stakeholders, potential investors, and industry leaders. Prior to the event, the CEO invests time in understanding the cultural norms and expectations of the attendees. They carefully choose appropriate attire, paying attention to details like personal grooming, ensuring they make a positive impression.

During the conference, the CEO engages in polite and respectful conversations, actively listening to others and expressing genuine interest in their perspectives. They follow proper dining etiquette during meals and graciously interact with attendees from different backgrounds. Through their exemplary behavior, the CEO builds strong connections, gains respect, and enhances the organization's reputation as a leader in the industry.

It's your turn now!

What steps will you take to put this trait into your leadership style?

By focusing on these essential traits and following the recommended action plans, you can develop and embed these qualities into your leadership style, ensuring your effectiveness in driving organizational success.

Steps to put the Key Traits to Practice, Embedding into your System

To embed these essential traits of extraordinary CEOs into your system and put them into practice, CEOs can follow a systematic approach that involves the following steps:

Self-Assessment: CEOs should start by conducting a thorough self-assessment to identify their strengths and areas for improvement related to the 14 traits. This can be done through self-reflection, seeking feedback from trusted advisors, or using assessments and tools designed for leadership development.

Step 1: Self-Assessment to Identify Strengths and Areas for Improvement

To conduct a thorough self-assessment and identify strengths and areas for improvement related to these traits, CEOs can follow these steps:

1. Reflect on Past Experiences: Take time to reflect on past experiences as a CEO and evaluate how you have demonstrated each of the 14 traits. Consider specific situations where you exhibited these traits effectively and those where there may have been room for improvement. Think about the outcomes and the impact of your actions.
2. Seek Feedback: Obtain feedback from trusted sources such as board members, executives, mentors, and employees. Ask for their honest perspectives on your strengths and areas for improvement related to the 14 traits. Their

insights can provide valuable perspectives and highlight blind spots that may not be apparent to you.

3. Use Assessment Tools: Utilize assessment tools specifically designed for leadership development and self-assessment. These tools may include personality assessments, 360-degree feedback surveys, or leadership competency assessments. They can provide structured insights into your leadership style, strengths, and potential areas for growth.
4. Conduct Self-Reflection: Engage in introspection and self-reflection exercises. Consider questions such as: What traits do I believe are my strengths as a CEO? In which areas do I feel I need improvement? What feedback have I received in the past that relates to these traits? What actions or behaviors align with the 14 traits that I can identify within myself?
5. Analyze Performance Data: Review performance data, such as key performance indicators (KPIs), employee engagement scores, and organizational metrics, to assess how your leadership style and behaviors have influenced organizational outcomes. Look for patterns or trends that can provide insights into your effectiveness in practicing the 14 traits.
6. Compare with Role Models: Identify CEOs or leaders whom you admire and consider their embodiment of the 14 traits. Compare their leadership style to your own and identify gaps or areas where you can align your behaviors more closely with these traits.

7. Engage in Peer Learning: Participate in CEO peer networks, forums, or mastermind groups where you can learn from and share experiences with other CEOs. Engaging in discussions and sharing challenges and successes can provide valuable perspectives and insights into how you stack up against the 14 traits.
8. Prioritize Areas for Improvement: Based on the insights gained from the self-assessment, prioritize the areas where you believe improvement would have the most significant impact on your effectiveness as a CEO. Focus on a few key traits at a time to avoid overwhelming yourself and to allow for meaningful growth.

Example: Let's take the trait "Excellent Communicator" as an example:

1. Reflect on Past Experiences: Recall instances where you effectively communicated your vision, goals, and expectations to employees, stakeholders, and the broader community. Consider situations where your communication may have fallen short or resulted in misunderstandings.
2. Seek Feedback: Approach key stakeholders, such as board members, employees, and trusted advisors, and request their feedback on your communication skills. Ask for specific examples of when your communication was particularly effective or could have been improved.
3. Use Assessment Tools: Complete a 360-degree feedback survey that evaluates your communication style and effectiveness. This

can provide a comprehensive view of your communication skills from multiple perspectives.

4. Conduct Self-Reflection: Take time for self-reflection and consider your own perception of your communication abilities. Analyze how well you articulate ideas, listen actively, and adapt your communication style to different audiences or situations.
5. Analyze Performance Data: Review organizational metrics related to communication, such as employee engagement scores, customer satisfaction ratings, or feedback from external stakeholders. Look for correlations between these metrics and your communication efforts.
6. Compare with Role Models: Identify CEOs or leaders known for their excellent communication skills. Observe their communication style, both in written and verbal forms, and assess how it compares to your own. Identify areas where you can learn from their example.
7. Engage in Peer Learning: Participate in CEO peer networks or forums focused on communication skills development. Engage in discussions and share experiences with other CEOs to learn from their communication successes and challenges.
8. Prioritize Areas for Improvement: Based on the insights gained, identify specific aspects of communication that you want to improve, such as active listening, delivering impactful presentations, or fostering effective two-way communication within the organization. Set

actionable goals and seek opportunities for growth in these areas.

By following these steps and applying them to each of the 14 traits, CEOs can gain a deeper understanding of their strengths and areas for improvement, enabling them to focus on personal and professional growth in alignment with these essential qualities.

Step 2: Goal Setting: Based on the self-assessment, CEOs should set specific and measurable goals for enhancing each trait. These goals should be aligned with their overall leadership development plan and the organization's strategic objectives.

Setting Specific and Measurable Goals

To set specific and measurable goals for enhancing each of the traits, while aligning them with the overall leadership development plan and the organization's strategic objectives, CEOs can follow these steps:

1. Identify Key Areas of Focus: Review the 14 traits and assess which areas require the most attention and improvement based on the organization's current challenges and future goals. Consider the strategic priorities of the organization and how each trait aligns with those objectives. Example: If the organization is undergoing a digital transformation, the CEO may prioritize traits such as adaptability and visionary thinking to drive innovation and navigate the changing landscape.
2. Define Clear Objectives: For each trait, clearly define the desired outcomes and behaviors that align with the organization's strategic objectives. Make sure the objectives are specific, measurable, achievable, relevant,

and time-bound (SMART goals). Example: For the trait of empowerment, the CEO may set an objective to delegate decision-making authority to department heads for 80% of non-strategic operational decisions within the next six months.

3. Break Goals into Actionable Steps: Determine the specific actions or milestones needed to achieve each goal. Break down the goals into smaller, actionable steps that can be tracked and measured over time. Example: To enhance the trait of excellent communication, the CEO may break the goal down into steps such as enrolling in a public speaking course, conducting monthly town hall meetings with employees, and implementing a feedback system to assess communication effectiveness.
4. Assign Responsibility and Accountability: Clearly define who will be responsible for executing each goal and establish accountability mechanisms to ensure progress and follow-through. Example: The CEO may assign responsibility to the Chief People Officer to oversee the implementation of initiatives related to employee empowerment and establish regular check-ins to monitor progress.
5. Align with Leadership Development Plan: Integrate the goals for enhancing the traits with the CEO's overall leadership development plan. Ensure that the goals align with the CEO's personal growth areas and professional development activities. Example: If the CEO has identified a need for improved

strategic thinking, they may incorporate reading strategic management books, attending relevant workshops, or seeking mentorship from seasoned strategic leaders as part of their development plan.

6. Monitor Progress and Adjust as Needed: Regularly review and track progress toward the goals for enhancing each trait. Collect data, feedback, and performance indicators to assess the effectiveness of the actions taken and make adjustments as necessary. Example: Conduct quarterly assessments to gauge progress in enhancing the trait of resilience, such as measuring employee engagement levels during challenging times or analyzing the organization's ability to adapt to market changes.

By following these steps, CEOs can set specific and measurable goals for enhancing each trait that are aligned with their leadership development plan and the organization's strategic objectives. This approach ensures that efforts to develop these traits are purposeful, targeted, and contribute to the overall success of both the CEO and the organization.

Step 3: Skill Development: CEOs can engage in targeted skill development activities to enhance each trait. This can include attending relevant workshops or conferences, enrolling in executive education programs, seeking mentorship from experienced leaders, or working with executive coaches who specialize in leadership development.

Engaging in Targeted Skill Development Activities

To engage in targeted skill development activities that enhance each trait while aligning with the CEO's overall leadership development plan and the organization's strategic objectives, CEOs can follow these steps:

1. Identify Skill Gaps: Assess the current skill set and identify areas where improvement is needed for each of the traits. Consider feedback from self-assessment, performance evaluations, and input from trusted advisors to pinpoint specific skill gaps. Example: If the CEO identifies a gap in their decision-making skills, they may need to develop the ability to gather and analyze data effectively, seek diverse perspectives, and make informed decisions efficiently.
2. Prioritize Skill Development: Determine which skills are most critical to the CEO's leadership role and the organization's strategic objectives. Prioritize skill development based on their potential impact on leadership effectiveness and alignment with organizational goals. Example: If the organization is expanding into new markets, the CEO may prioritize skill development in cross-cultural communication and global business acumen.
3. Research Development Opportunities: Explore targeted skill development activities that align with the identified skill gaps and strategic objectives. This can include executive education programs, workshops, seminars, industry conferences, online courses, coaching, or mentoring opportunities. Example: If the CEO wants to enhance their financial planning skills, they may enroll in a financial management program offered by a

reputable business school or seek guidance from a financial advisor or mentor.

4. Develop a Personalized Development Plan: Create a personalized development plan that outlines specific skill development goals, activities, and timelines. Align these goals with the CEO's overall leadership development plan and the organization's strategic objectives. Example: The CEO may set a goal to improve their negotiation skills by attending a negotiation skills workshop within the next three months and practicing negotiation techniques in real-world scenarios during team meetings.
5. Allocate Resources: Allocate resources, including time, budget, and organizational support, to enable the CEO's skill development activities. Ensure that these resources align with the organization's strategic priorities and demonstrate a commitment to leadership development. Example: The organization may provide a budget for executive education programs, allocate dedicated time for skill development activities, and assign a mentor or coach to support the CEO's growth.
6. Implement Learning and Application: Engage actively in the chosen skill development activities and apply the acquired knowledge and skills in real-world situations. Seek opportunities within the organization to practice and reinforce the newly acquired skills. Example: After attending a workshop on strategic thinking, the CEO can apply strategic frameworks and analysis techniques to

evaluate new business opportunities or create a strategic roadmap for the organization.

7. Seek Feedback and Evaluation: Regularly seek feedback from trusted advisors, peers, and employees to assess progress and effectiveness in applying the newly developed skills. Use this feedback to refine and adjust skill development efforts as needed. Example: The CEO may request feedback from direct reports on their delegation and empowerment skills to gauge their progress and identify areas for further improvement.

By following these steps, CEOs can engage in targeted skill development activities that enhance each trait, align with their overall leadership development plan, and support the organization's strategic objectives. This deliberate approach ensures that skill development efforts are purposeful, impactful, and contribute to the CEO's growth as a leader and the organization's success.

Step 4: Building a Supportive Environment: CEOs should create a supportive environment within the organization that encourages the development and practice of the 14 traits. This can be achieved by fostering a culture of learning and growth, promoting open communication, and recognizing and rewarding behaviors that align with these traits.

Creating a Supportive Environment that Encourages the Development and Practice

To create a supportive environment within the organization that encourages the development and practice of the 14 traits and fosters a culture of learning and growth, CEOs can follow these steps:

1. Clarify and Communicate Expectations: Clearly articulate the importance of the 14

traits and how they align with the organization's values, mission, and strategic objectives. Communicate these expectations consistently through various channels such as town hall meetings, internal communications, and employee on-boarding processes. Example: The CEO can emphasize the significance of traits like empowerment and strategic thinking by highlighting their impact on innovation, employee engagement, and overall organizational success.

2. Lead by Example: CEOs should model the behaviors associated with the 14 traits in their own actions, decisions, and interactions. Demonstrate authenticity, integrity, and continuous growth, inspiring others to follow suit. Example: The CEO can empower teams by delegating authority, actively seeking input from employees, and providing opportunities for growth and development.
3. Foster a Culture of Learning: Promote a culture of continuous learning and growth by providing resources, training programs, and learning opportunities that support the development of the 14 traits. Encourage employees at all levels to engage in professional development and knowledge-sharing activities. Example: The CEO can establish a learning and development budget to support employees' participation in workshops, conferences, and online courses that focus on enhancing the identified traits.
4. Encourage Open Communication: Create an environment where open and transparent communication is valued. Encourage

employees to share ideas, concerns, and feedback. Foster a safe space for open dialogue, where diverse perspectives are welcomed and respected. Example: The CEO can implement regular forums, such as team meetings, town halls, or suggestion platforms, where employees feel comfortable sharing their thoughts, ideas, and suggestions related to the 14 traits.

5. Recognize and Reward Behaviors: Implement recognition and reward systems that celebrate and reinforce behaviors aligned with the 14 traits. Acknowledge and appreciate individuals and teams who consistently demonstrate these qualities, fostering a positive reinforcement loop. Example: The CEO can establish an employee recognition program that specifically acknowledges and rewards employees who exemplify traits such as tenacity, excellent communication, or ethical decision-making.
6. Provide Development Opportunities: Offer development opportunities that directly support the cultivation of the 14 traits. This can include mentoring programs, leadership workshops, cross-functional projects, or stretch assignments that allow employees to practice and develop these qualities. Example: The CEO can create a mentorship program where experienced leaders mentor employees to develop their leadership skills, including traits like empowerment and strategic thinking.
7. Evaluate and Adjust Organizational Policies: Regularly review and assess existing organizational policies and practices to ensure

they align with the desired traits. Make adjustments or creat and advancement processes to consider these qualities as important factors.

By following these steps, CEOs can create a supportive environment that fosters the development and practice of the 14 traits. This environment encourages employees at all levels to embrace these qualities, contributing to a culture of learning, growth, and high-performance within the organization.

Step 5: Modeling Behaviors: CEOs should lead by example and model the behaviors associated with each trait. By consistently demonstrating the traits in their own actions, decision-making, and interactions with others, CEOs set the tone for the organization and inspire their teams to follow suit.

Step 6: Integration into Hiring and Talent Development: CEOs can embed the 14 traits into the organization's hiring and talent development processes. They can incorporate assessment tools, interview questions, and performance criteria that align with these traits to ensure that they are valued and sought after in potential candidates and existing employees.

Step 7: Ongoing Evaluation and Feedback: CEOs should regularly evaluate their progress in developing and practicing the 14 traits. This can be done through self-assessment, seeking feedback from stakeholders, and conducting performance reviews that include a focus on leadership qualities. Adjustments and additional development efforts can be made based on these evaluations.

Example: Let's take the trait "Empowering" as an example:

Plan:

- ✓ Goal: Enhance the trait of empowerment to create a culture of autonomy, creativity, and innovation within the organization.
- ✓ Timeline: 12 months.

Action Steps:

1. Conduct a self-assessment to identify current strengths and areas for improvement related to empowerment.
2. Enroll in a leadership development program focused on empowering leadership styles.
3. Engage in regular one-on-one meetings with team members to discuss their goals and provide them with the necessary resources and support.
4. Delegate decision-making authority to capable team members, allowing them to take ownership of projects and initiatives.
5. Create a platform for idea sharing and innovation, such as an internal innovation hub or suggestion system.
6. Recognize and reward employees who demonstrate empowered behaviors and generate impactful ideas.
7. Incorporate empowerment as a core competency in the organization's performance review process.
8. Provide ongoing training and development opportunities to enhance employees' skills and confidence in decision-making.
9. Seek feedback from team members on their experience of empowerment within the organization and make adjustments as needed.
10. Communicate the importance of empowerment and its benefits to the

organization's overall success through internal communications channels.

By following these steps and adapting them to each of the traits, CEOs can systematically integrate and practice these qualities, creating a culture that fosters exceptional leadership and drives organizational success.

Conclusion

Congratulations on completing the insightful journey through **'The CEO's 31-Day Power Plan: Unlocking Success through Essential Traits'** You have embarked on a transformative exploration of the traits and attributes that define exceptional CEOs and leaders. As you reach the conclusion of this book, it is important to reflect on the valuable lessons learned and the impact they can have on your leadership journey.

Throughout these pages, you have delved into the core elements that drive success in the realm of leadership. From visionary thinking and strategic mindset to effective communication, resilience, and beyond, you have gained a comprehensive understanding of the traits necessary to excel as a CEO.

Remember that true growth and development require continuous effort and application. It is not enough to merely possess knowledge; you must actively integrate these traits into your leadership style, decisions, and interactions. Embrace the journey of self-improvement and make a conscious effort to embody these essential traits in your daily actions and behaviors.

As you move forward, seek opportunities to refine your leadership capabilities and engage in lifelong learning. Surround yourself with mentors, coaches, and a supportive network that challenges and inspires you. Embrace feedback, both positive and constructive, as it provides valuable insights into areas for growth and improvement.

Never underestimate the influence of your leadership on those around you. By embodying these essential traits, you have the power to motivate, inspire, and create positive change within your organization. As you continue to cultivate your own leadership excellence, extend your knowledge and support to others, fostering a culture of growth and empowerment.

Remember that leadership is a continuous journey, and the traits explored in this book are not limited to a finite set. They serve as a foundation for your growth as a leader, but they are not the endpoint. Embrace the ever-evolving nature of leadership and remain open to new experiences, ideas, and perspectives. Continue to invest in your personal and professional development, always striving for greater heights.

As you close the final pages of this book, carry the wisdom and insights gained with you on your continued path to leadership excellence. Embrace the responsibility and privilege of being a CEO, knowing that your dedication to personal growth and the embodiment of these essential traits will have a profound impact on your organization, your team, and yourself.

Thank you for joining us on this transformative journey. We wish you continued success and fulfillment as you unleash the power within and make a lasting difference in the world through your exceptional leadership.

May your journey as a CEO be one of continuous growth, purpose, and remarkable achievements!

About the Author 'GERARD ASSEY'

Gerard Assey is a Graduate in Economics, a PGD in Management (HRD) and holds a Doctorate in Leadership. Gerard holds several International Qualifications in Sales, Debt Collection, Training & Teaching, and is a 'Fellow' of the prestigious 'Institute of Sales & Marketing Management'-UK, a Certified NLP Practitioner, a 'Certified Trainer', an 'Accredited Management Teacher-Behavioral Sciences', a 'Certified Competency Facilitator', a 'Certified Management Consultant'- (the International credentials of a professional management consultant, awarded in accordance with global standards of the ICMCI); and a Certification from the University of Michigan in 'Successful Negotiation: Essential Strategies and Skills'

He is also a Member of the 'National Association of Sales Professionals' backed with several years experience in varied industries, both in India and Overseas. He also holds an 'Etiquette Consultant' Certification from the USA (by Sue Fox, Author of Best Seller: 'Business Etiquette for Dummies'. She has trained some of the top celebrities' world over). He was also a recipient of a scholarship for extensive training in Japan on 'Corporate Management for India'.

Gerard Assey is 'Founder & Chief Corporate Trainer' of the Group: **'Citius, Altius, Fortius Unlimited'**- an organization that **celebrated 20 years of Glorious Service** in 2021, focusing on 3 Core Competencies:

People. Performance. Profit; in functional areas of Sales & Marketing, HR & Organizational Development, covering Recruitment, Training & Consultancy!

Having managed organizations with large Sales Forces in India & Overseas, his specialization cover extensive areas of Sales Training (All levels - Presentation, Negotiation, Key/ Strategic Accounts Management & Managerial Skills for all sectors), Bid Proposal/ Capture Planning/ Management Trainings, Retail Sales, Customer Service & Customer Retention Programs, Training for Prevention & Collection of Debt, Self & Personal Development Programs (Time Management, Teamwork & Team Building, Business Etiquette & Personal Grooming, Leadership & Managerial Skills, People Management Skills, Train-the-Trainer etc), including preparation of Custom-designed Business Manuals for Internal (HR, Induction, and Sales etc) & External use (Instruction, User Manuals).

Gerard has successfully conducted over 6000 Trainings & Workshops (as of Nov '23) all across India, Middle East, Africa, Europe & S.E. Asia. Besides public programs conducted regularly, both in India & Overseas, he has some of the top names as clients whom he services from Single Owners to large Public & Government undertakings, covering all sectors, for their in-house needs.

His website: www.CollectionSkills.com is the only one in this part of the world to be featured in the 'Collections & Credit Risk Magazine-USA' under 'Who's Who in Training' and ranks TOP, along with other websites listed below on most search engines.

Gerard is author of 92 books already (Nov 2023),

A few of our business related books:

1. Bite-sized Bits on Commonsense Management
2. Heart to Heart on Life's Principles'
3. How to become a Successful Manager
4. The Sales Professionals' Master Workbook of S.Y.S.T.E.M.S
5. The Professional Business Email Etiquette Handbook & Guide
6. The Professional Business Video-Conferencing Etiquette Handbook & Guide
7. Professional Presentation Skills
8. Exceptional Customer Service
9. Professional Tele-Marketing Skills
10. Professional Debt Collection Skills
11. The G.R.E.A.T. Sales & Service Workbook
12. Sales Training Advantage for Results (*The Ultimate Sales Training Manual to enable you stand out as a S.T.A.R.*)
13. CEO Daily Planner & Organizer
14. The Sales Professionals' Master Daily Planner
15. The Professional Debt Collector's Master Daily Planner
16. My Daily Planner & Organizer
17. MY EMERGENCY INFORMATION RECORD (Family Emergency & Peace of Mind Planner)
18. The Ultimate Therapist & Counselors Planner and Organizer
19. Building an Ethical Workplace
20. Managing Relationships at Work
21. Managing Business Meetings Effectively
22. Effective Delegation Skills
23. Goal Setting for Success
24. B2B Selling by Email
25. Professional Business Etiquette & Grooming
26. Dining Etiquette & Table Manners
27. Effective Networking Skills
28. Grooming, Etiquette & Manners for Teens, Young Adults & Future Leaders
29. Inter-Personal Skills
30. Get Ready, Get Hired!
31. Selling in a Recession
32. Effective Receivables Management in an Economic Downturn!
33. Real Estate & Property Sales Training
34. Credit Sales & Accounts Receivable Management
35. Selling Skills for Real Estate & Property Advisors
36. Take G.R.E.A.T. C.A.R.E!

37. Spa, Salon & Health Club Selling Skills
38. Selling Travel, Holiday & MICE Services
39. Selling Skills for Spa's, Salons & Health Clubs
40. Retailing in Salons & Spas
41. Selling Holiday, Vacation, Tours & Packages
42. The Power of Sales Referrals
43. Selling Luxury
44. Technical Selling Skills
45. Financial Advisors Sales Training
46. Dealing with Burnout at Work Monopolize Your Markets
47. Selling to Affluent Customers
48. Growing up with Grace
49. Financial Selling Skills
50. *The Effective Manager's Guide: Key Skills to Thrive*
51. From Aspiring to Inspiring: A Guide for New Managers on the Rise
52. The Power of Focus
53. Selling with Integrity: Sell Like Jesus The Perfect Role Model!
54. 31 Habits of Champions: Your 31-Day Journey to Greatness
55. Rejecting Grasshopper Talk: From Grasshopper to Giant-Killer-*Defeating Giants Daily!*
56. Navigate the AI-Powered Future of Bid & Proposals: Up-Skill to Stay Relevant with Alternative Career Paths & Opportunities
57. Hiring Sales Winners
58. Present with Impact
59. Success Unlocked: *Breaking Free from Habits that Hold You Back*
60. Complaints to Cheers, Feedback to Gold: Mastering Complaints Management
61. Thriving Together: *Cultivating Diversity, Equity, and Inclusion*
62. Coaching Skills for Sales Managers
63. Soaring to Success in Business & Leadership: Swifter, Higher, Stronger!
64. From Classroom to Podium: A Student's Guide to Powerful Public Speaking & Presentation Skills
65. Developing Self-Discipline
66. The CEO's 31-Day Power Plan: Unlocking Success through Essential Traits

Besides regularly contributing to business & trade journals, including international ones such as the 'Creative Training Techniques' and the 'Sales News' of the U.S.A, He is also a member of several prestigious bodies & trade associations, having participated in many Conferences & Workshops in India & Overseas.

Prior to his last assignment of leading & managing a large MNC as head, Gerard had a 3-year stint in the Middle East as a Consultant with a leading British Consultancy Firm.

As the past 'Official Country Representative' for the International Business Award- 'THE STEVIES'-(the business world's own Oscar) for about 4 years- he ensured a few Indian companies that qualify for the same every year!

Gerard can be contacted at:
Email: training@Sales-Training.in,training@CollectionSkills.com
Websites:

www.Sales-Training.in
www.EtiquetteWorks.in
www.CollectionSkills.com
www.RetailSalesTraining.in
www.SalesTrainingIndia.com
www.ManualPreparation.com
www.TrainingWithPuppets.com
www.FirstContactAcademy.com
www.SalesAndMarketingRecruiter.com

Our TRAININGS that can help your team

- ✓ **Sales Effectiveness**: Selling Skills for any Sector: Service/ Logistics/ FMCG Realty/ Insurance & Finance/ Media/ SPA's, Health Clubs & Salons/ Key Account Management, Effective Negotiation Skills/ Bid & Proposal Management Skills/ Retail Sales Training: Any Sector (Auto, Jewelry, Clothing, Luxury etc)
- ✓ **Customer Service Skills**-Complaints Handling & Customer Retention
- ✓ **Debt Prevention & Collection Skills**
- ✓ **Etiquette & Grooming**
- ✓ **Leadership & Managerial Skills**
- ✓ **Self & Personal Development Skills**: Presentation Skills/ Effective Communication Skills/Business Proposal Writing Skills/ Problem Solving & Decision Making Skills/ Empowering Secretaries-The perfect PA! (For Secretaries & PA's)/ Effective Time Management/ Teamwork & Teambuilding/ P.R.I.D.E- **P**ersonal **R**esponsibility **I**n **D**elivering **E**xcellence

www.ingramcontent.com/pod-product-compliance
Lightning Source LLC
Chambersburg PA
CBHW062110160726
48282CB00026B/745
* 9 7 8 9 3 9 2 4 9 2 7 4 7 *